Travelling Along

A STUDY COURSE

John Pritchard and John Simmonds

Illustrations by Ross Thomson

SCM PRESS LTD · LONDON

All rights reserved. No part of this publication may be reproduced, stored in a retrieval system, or transmitted, in any form or by any means, electronic, mechanical, photocopying, recording or otherwise, without the prior permission of the publisher, SCM Press Ltd.

Text © John Pritchard and John Simmonds 1982

Illustrations © Ross Thomson 1982

Design by Hickey Press Ltd

334 01680 0

First published 1982
by SCM Press Ltd
58 Bloomsbury Street, London WC1

Typeset by Willmer Brothers Limited
and printed in Great Britain by
Pindar Print Ltd, Scarborough

Contents

	About this book	4
1	Looking in the mirror	7
2	What kind of world do we live in?	10
3	What do people really value?	14
4	Why are we here?	16
5	Another dimension	20
6	Exploring together	22
7	Finding out more about Jesus	27
8	It's all in the Bible!	34
9	Exploring the Gospels	37
10	Jesus in his day	40
11	Jesus in every generation	45
12	Jesus our contemporary	48
13	The disciples of Jesus: then and now	52
14	Programme for tomorrow	59
	References and acknowledgements	64

About this book

Every day we spend a great deal of time reacting to immediate questions, like

>'What shall I wear?'
>'What's for tea?'
>'Where shall we go for our holidays?'
>'What's on TV?'
>'Have you seen Auntie lately?'
>'Can we afford a new . . .?'

All good questions, but sometimes it's worthwhile to consider more basic questions like

>'Who am I?'
>'What should I do?'
>'What kind of world do we want?'
>'What's the meaning of life?'
>'Why bother about these basic questions anyway?'

This book aims . . . to open up such questions and help people

>to discern in the way of Jesus a pattern for living.
>to share a common life with others committed to the quest.
>to engage in Christian actions with other people of goodwill

It assumes . . . that its readers are already involved in groups with some experience of Christian celebration, teaching and action. It is not a comprehensive guide to Christian teaching and living, for there's so much to discuss that is not written here.

Those who do not belong to a group would find it helpful to work through the book with someone else, for its authors believe that the best way to grow in understanding is to share insights.

Its approach . . . is to raise issues and to ask questions; the group's answers will provide the chief illumination. Members of the group are encouraged to introduce their own insights for consideration by the group. All group leaders should participate fully as members of the group, and not as outsiders, by virtue of their expertise or ordination! It is not assumed that one chapter will necessarily take only one session.

It can be used . . . in many settings, e.g. student societies, confirmation groups, house-groups, and so on. The best results will be achieved if people of a variety of interest and experience participate. Meetings of the like-minded have more limited horizons.

One more step along the world I go,
One more step along the world I go,
From the old things to the new
Keep me travelling along with you.
    And it's from the old I travel to the new,
    Keep me travelling along with you.

Round the corners of the world I turn,
More and more about the world I learn.
And the new things that I see
You'll be looking at along with me
    And it's from the old I travel to the new,
    Keep me travelling along with you.

As I travel through the bad and good
Keep me travelling the way I should.
Where I see no way to go
You'll be telling me the way, I know.
    And it's from the old I travel to the new,
    Keep me travelling along with you.

Give me courage when the world is rough,
Keep me loving though the world is tough.
Leap and sing in all I do,
Keep me travelling along with you.
    And it's from the old I travel to the new,
    Keep me travelling along with you.

You are older than the world can be,
You are younger than the life in me.
Ever old and ever new,
Keep me travelling along with you.
    And it's from the old I travel to the new,
    Keep me travelling along with you.

Sydney Carter

1 Looking in the mirror

It's important to realize

that your decisions and beliefs are in part affected by the sort of person you are,
and by the kind of people with whom you live.

There's nothing wrong in that, but remember that it is so.

We are all made up of a combination of

Hereditary factors
passed on from our parents (not only physical attributes, like the colour of our skin, but also our attitudes and ideas).

Environmental factors
coming to us from our neighbourhood, friendships, TV, radio, nationality, etc.

A real independent self
the 'real me', who can either accept or rebel against hereditary and environmental pressures.

When you think about the meaning of life and about how to live as a Christian, it will depend in part upon the kind of person you are.

So we begin by looking in the mirror!

Use the following questions, and see if you can discover

Who you are.
What made you the kind of person you are.
What you expect of life, and what life demands of you.

1 What is your name (proper names and nick-names)? Why are you called by these names?

2 Who belongs to your family (those in your house and those who live away)?

3 What do other people expect of you?

Your parents?
Your children?
Your brothers and sisters?
Teachers or bosses?
Friends?
People who work with you, or for you?
The Government?

4 What do you expect of other people? (use the same list again)

5 Are your ambitions for yourself the same as other people's for you?

6 What are your dreams (and your nightmares!)
   for yourself?
   for your country?
   for the world?

7 What makes you happy?

8 What upsets you?

9 Make a list of people whom you admire, and explain why you admire them.

10 Here is the hardest question of all! What sort of person are you?
   Do you have fixed ideas?
   Do you get on well with other people?
   Are you adaptable? How do you react to the unexpected?
   Are you hard-working?
   Are you a fighter? Will you put yourself out for something you really want?
   Are you generous?

11 No! Here's the hardest question of all. Do other people agree with your answers to question 10?!

2 What kind of world do we live in?

Some people say

that the world is ugly and cruel; others, that it is a beautiful place.
that the world is rich; others, that it is poor.
that it will last for ever; others, that its days are numbered.

All sorts of things affect our lives

global issues, like the energy crisis.
national issues, like unemployment.
local issues, like education policy.

Ask yourself

What really matters to my family?
        to my employers or school teachers?
        to my friends?
        to the Government?

Also, think of someone who is *very* different from you, and ask what really matters to them.

Remember who you are and keep asking questions!

To understand the world we live in, we must think hard and often about these questions. Today's answers may seem quite irrelevant tomorrow, when something else has cropped up; for we live in a world where changes happen at a hectic and ever-increasing rate. Also, what is important in Sheffield may appear insignificant in Aberdeen, and totally irrelevant in Sri Lanka. To get things in perspective, remember that you are not only a British citizen; you are a European, and a member of the human race, as well as a member of your local community. Sooner or later we are all students, workers, voters, consumers, pensioners . . .

What are the most significant issues for the world today?

Wealth and poverty?

For about £50 a year you can feed, clothe and educate a child in Bangladesh. But that is more than most people there see in a year.

Advancing technology?

Micro-electronics are transforming Western society. The potential uses and abuses are tremendous.

Population growth?

There will be twice as many people around by the year 2000; can they all be fed?

The arms race?

The USA and USSR possess enough nuclear weapons to wipe out the world many times over. Smaller 'conventional' weapons are sold in vast quantities to small countries who cannot afford them. We spend about 50% of our world research and development budget on arms.

Race conflict?

The colour of your skin is something you can neither change nor conceal – which makes discrimination or oppression, based on colour, especially vile.

The energy crisis?

We are rapidly running out of non-renewable fuels, and raping the planet in the process.

Can you think of any more issues?

Now ask yourself

What's the *worst* that could happen as a result of these issues?
What's the *best* that could happen?
What would ensure that the best happens and not the worst?

Freedom of conscience and speech?

In Communist and non-Communist countries alike, more people than ever before are imprisoned for their religious or political beliefs.

Please don't skip these questions, for it has been said that the greatest threat to mankind is that people just don't care enough to put themselves out:
    the optimists blindly assume that it will all work out in the end;
    the pessimists are overwhelmed by their own sense of impotence.

In each case, apathy and inertia are the result, and that's the greatest enemy.

Perhaps it depends on our perspective. Are these enormous issues problems or challenges?

3 What do people really value?

The things that matter

Try placing these items in order of importance:

Freedom

People want to be able to choose for themselves and not to be dictated to by anyone.

Belonging

People need to belong to a group or community. They need to love and to be loved. We 'belong' at many levels: marriage, family, school, work, neighbourhood, friendships, club, nation, EEC, etc.

Survival

People need food, fuel, clothing, and shelter, just to stay alive.

Education

People need the means to communicate (reading and writing); they want a chance to develop their skills and intellect (training); and to grow in understanding (discernment).

Money

People have a desire to own things; a place to call their own. Money is a means to ownership.

Health

People want an environment free from disease, and medical care when they are ill. They need a healthy diet and life-style.

Religion

People feel a need to explore the meaning of the universe and their place within it. Their response is expressed in worship and celebration.

Culture

People find their deepest feelings expressed in art, music, literature, TV, films, sports, etc.

Sex

People long to express deep feelings sexually. Human sexuality is a capacity for total self-giving and fulfilment in relationship with another.

Me

Besides all other values, people place a value upon themselves as individuals. They seek their own welfare. Sometimes a person wants to be powerful, sometimes dependent; sometimes the boss, sometimes the servant.

Can you think of anything else which is important to groups and individuals?

Can you think of anyone who is deprived of these things?

4 Why are we here?

If we think about it, we soon realize that there are a great many different aspects to our life because at one time or another we find ourselves in quite varied roles. People may regard us as

    shopper
    gardener
    neighbour
    viewer
    daughter
    student
    passenger
    reader
    youth club member

not to mention whatever we may list on an official form as 'occupation'

Every role brings us into relationship with other people:

Drink a cup of tea in a café and you are brought into relationship with a waitress, who earns a wage; with a café owner, who has his overheads to cover; with transport workers; plantation owners; and the tea-pickers in Sri Lanka or India whose meagre living keeps them in dire poverty. One could go further and say that the selfsame cup of tea links us with ambitious and greedy colonizers, our forebears, and a twentieth-century system which perpetuates exploitation.

Roles involve both *direct* contact: shopper with shopkeeper,
daughter with parent,
student with teacher;

and *indirect* contact: a reader with a writer;
a daughter, not only with parents, but also with uncles, grandparents, and even more remote ancestors.

We may not have inherited much money from great-great-grandma, but we certainly possess some of her genes!

Some of these roles are freely chosen: e.g. a TV viewer (you can always switch off!). In some, you have no say: e.g. no one asked you if you wanted to be someone's child. Gardening can be either a regrettable necessity or an enjoyable pastime; it depends who you are.

Make a list of all the roles you fill

Which have you chosen?
Which have been imposed upon you?
Which do you enjoy the most?   Why?
Which would you most like to give up?   Why?

Now let's focus on one particular activity

> – your role as a reader of this book . . .
> You haven't given up yet!
> Who does it bring you into contact with?

Why do you belong to your group?

> Is it because your friends go?
> > because someone persuaded you to join?
> > because you feel you can help the other members?
> > because you want to know more about Christianity?
> > because the group has been formed to consider confirmation or church membership?

What do you feel about belonging to a church?

> Christians have been called a lot of names:
> 'saints' and 'hypocrites';
> 'do-gooders' and 'trouble-makers';
> 'soldiers' and 'bigots';
> 'pilgrims' and 'cranks';
> 'friendly' and 'cliquish';
> 'apprentices' . . .
>
> 'Apprentices' – yes!
> That's what the word 'disciple' (Latin – *discipulus*) means: 'a learner'.
>
> What name would you choose for yourself?   Why?

What made you interested in the church?

You were taken as a baby to be baptized (or dedicated); then you went to Sunday School or Junior Church, and to Youth Fellowship. You have grown up in the church, you have always belonged.

You have no family association with the church (even if you were baptized as a child). You started going to the youth club with your friends; the youth services are good fun; now you're going to more serious, thoughtful meetings, too.

One day you heard an interview with an evangelist on the radio; something struck you about him, and you went along to his meeting. Your whole life changed that night – you were converted; ever since, you've been trying to learn more about Jesus, and to live in his way.

Your neighbour was very kind when your wife was ill; the minister was very attentive when she died. People invited you to a house group and, since you were lonely, you started going.

What's your story?   *Why are you here?*

5 Another dimension

Why are you here?

Family reasons, friendships, coincidences and other personal circumstances are only part of the answer. To deal with the question fully brings in another dimension.

Christians believe that there is more to reality than the visible, tangible experiences of life. Along with religious people of every age and culture they talk about the activity of God: in themselves, in others, in the world. In this way they attempt to make sense of the world and explore the principles that guide and explain human affairs and destinies.

Why are you here at all?

Where does God come into your answer?

To believe in God is not peculiar to Christians. What distinguishes Christians – of whatever denomination – from Jews, Hindus and other religious communities, is their relationship to Jesus of Nazareth (about 6 BC–AD 30).

They would not all describe this relationship in the same way:

> Some describe personal experiences of 'Jesus – alive today!'. They claim direct contact with him – through conversion, prayer, and the Bible.

> Some have a close affinity with the attitudes and values which Jesus set out in his teaching and demonstrated by his actions.

> Some believe that the church today possesses special insights and powers which were given to the first Christians by Jesus, and have been passed on down the centuries.

> All believe that, in some way, Jesus helps them understand the meaning of life, by teaching them about God and how they should respond to God.

From the very beginning, unfortunately, some people have claimed to be the ' true ' Christians. In the conviction that they alone were right, they have outlawed one another, and indeed persecuted those who disagreed with them. Thus new denominations came to be formed. Today, Christians still find it impossible to agree on many things.

And yet, even in their disagreements they have something in common – they all claim to have special knowledge of Jesus. For it is in proclaiming what they believe about Jesus that they squabble!

Why do Christians come to different conclusions?

It has something to do with *who* they are;
- *what* circumstances they live in;
- *whom* they live amongst;
- *how* they read the Bible;
- *how* they respond to what other Christians say;
- *what* really matters to them at the time;

and so on . . .

What factors influence the way you think about God and Jesus?

6 Exploring together

So far, we have considered who we are, and how we relate to other people; we have considered what people value in life, and what issues we all face.

But still we face even more basic questions, like

> 'What's the meaning of life?'
>
> 'Why are we here at all?'
>
> 'Is there more to life than just eating, living and working?'

People keep asking these questions; philosophers return to them again and again; followers of many religions explore all their hopes, fears and beliefs in stories, doctrines, symbols, images, liturgies, and so on.

Setting out

It's useful to think of members of a Christian group as explorers . . . a bit like Christopher Columbus and his men, setting out on a voyage of discovery.

Just imagine what it was like at the time of Columbus. People really believed that the world was flat; go too far north, south, east, or west and you would meet your end! Everyone knew that, and yet a crack-pot called Columbus got hooked on the idea that the world was really a globe – a ball spinning in space; go in any direction and you would return to your starting point. So in 1492, he set sail westwards from Europe to reach the East Indies. He had no chart, and no certainty. He lived by a hunch. No doubt he had times when he thought his journey would end in disaster; certainly there were people even in his crew who said he was mad.

Columbus was one of those rare people who nurtured a creative urge to push back the frontiers of human experience: to leave well-charted waters and to sail dangerously. He was more than an adventurer; he was an innovator, for he helped change the contemporary view of reality.

Let's take a cue from Christopher Columbus, and imagine what his approach could mean for us in our search for meaning.

Our journey is undertaken in a company of friends

> people who are concerned to find meaning in life;
> people in the church group where we are;
> people of other beliefs;
> people of no belief.

When we are confident of our insights, we can share our convictions with others; in doubt or despair, we can draw on the reservoir of other people's faith and experience.

Sometimes the church will be a strength to us; sometimes it may hinder our exploration. But all the time we should allow God's creative spirit to shape our perspectives, and even to reform the church!

Ways of exploring

Down the centuries, people have used a multitude of tools in the religious quest. Amongst them, prayer has held a special place – prayer in private, and prayer in groups; different forms of prayer, reflecting different attitudes to God:

> some seek mercy at the feet of an eternal Judge;
> some ask the Great Controller to intervene in special ways for particular people;
> some ask for guidance from a God who directs the lives of nations and individuals;
> some reflect on the mystery of a God who sustains and supports all life, hidden in the depths of existence;
> some find comfort and forgiveness from a God who waits like the father of the wayward son.

Though such prayers are very different, all of them explore the nature of God. They express what people believe about God: the background to our search.

More than prayer

Besides prayer, other tools are available to us – other ways of exploring:

> talking to each other;
> listening to preachers and reading books;
> getting involved in activities, which put our ideas into practice;
> responding with awareness and interest to all we see, touch, or hear: pictures, places, people, poems, songs, machines, nature.

Some of those tools are available within the church – in its celebration and worship. Some must be sought outside the church. Some will be peculiarly our own.

Our search will be closely related to our understanding of God

Some people believe that God is the Final Controller of everything – people, planets, and galaxies.

> God is in charge of events;
> God made the world and keeps it going;
> God made us and plans our lives;
> God never changes – consistent and strong;
> God expects us to fit in with a pre-ordained way of doing things: whilst we may disobey, we will only be happy when we respond positively. We should set aside our own wishes and acknowledge his authority.

This is a God who is above, beyond and outside us. It is the traditional Jewish/Christian view of God. It uses specific names to describe God, like Creator, Eternal, All-Knowing, Almighty, Lord, King, Judge, and so on. Many human institutions have mirrored such beliefs about what God is like, e.g. the emperor, the king, the headmaster, the priest, the Victorian father, the State.

Other people think of God as a creative spirit, discerned in the changes and growth of the universe, the arts and sciences, human relationships, individual development and understanding. A God 'in whom we live and move and have our being'. So it is hard to describe just where the life of God begins and ends, for he is inseparable from the world, present everywhere. Growth, change and development are essential to God's nature. God is not above or outside, but within us – the ground upon which we build.

God shows himself in many ways

With such diverse views (expressed not only within Christianity, but also in other great religions – compare Islam and Buddhism, for example) it will be no surprise to discover that we can speak of God in many ways. Sometimes we'll journey in familiar places, and we'll feel safe and happy; at other times our pilgrimage will take us to strange places with few landmarks. Sometimes we may think we are approaching our journey's end, only to be infuriated when we find that our expected destination was but another signpost, driving us deeper into the unknown.

Some more questions

1. What kind of group do we belong to?
   Does it help or hinder true discovery and search?
   Are we prepared to be honest with each other, and to learn from one another?

2. Can you think of a prayer which means nothing to you?
   means a great deal to you?

3. Share with the group anything which helps you to appreciate life more, e.g. a story, a picture, a special place or time, some music, etc.

4. If someone asked you to tell them about God, what would you say?

7 Finding out more about Jesus

Christianity is based on the life of Jesus. It is a movement inspired by a man who lived in Palestine during the Roman occupation.

Who was he?

Some say, 'He was a very special man; the finest who ever lived.'
Some say, 'He was God-alive-on-earth.'
Some say, 'He was a prophet, with remarkable insights into life, and a wonderful way with people.'

What do you think about him?

Do any of the pictures here correspond to your idea of Jesus?
Do any offend you?

Can you think of a hymn, a poem, or a quotation which describes Jesus for you?
What word comes into your head when you hear the name 'Jesus'?
Saviour... Lord... Superstar... Friend...   Now you have a go!

But why consider Jesus anyway?

Christians have had many disagreements; their beliefs and experiences have been very diverse; yet they have all agreed that Jesus of Nazareth is supremely important in our search for meaning, and in our attempt to know God.

However, we must be careful to check whether our own views are reasonable or pure fantasy. It's all too easy to invent the kind of Jesus we want! So we must look back into history to see what we can discover.

Where can we look?

1 The letters of Paul

It is generally agreed that the very first followers of Jesus did not leave behind detailed accounts of him. So the earliest written references to him that we find are in the letters of Paul, at second hand.

Paul never met Jesus, and the first that we hear of him is as a fierce opponent of the church, involved in a minor way in the stoning of Stephen, the first Christian martyr. There is an account of his conversion and later activity in the second half of the Acts of the Apostles. Paul was a champion of Christianity for the Gentiles; he argued that it was not necessary to be circumcised, and become a Jew before you became a Christian, as some more conservative members of the church believed. Although he is often remembered as the man who thought women should keep quiet in church, in fact in many respects he saw more clearly than anyone else in his day the consequences of the life, teaching, death and resurrection of Jesus.

Paul carried Jesus' teaching on and applied it far-sightedly to new situations, yet remarkably enough he says comparatively little about the life of Jesus and quotes hardly anything that Jesus said. He talks far more about the risen Christ who met him on the Damascus road. However, if we look carefully through the letters he wrote to the young churches that he helped to found, we do see a number of references to Jesus, and particularly to the Last Supper and the Resurrection. Here are the most important of them. Can you find them in your New Testament? If you get stuck, you will find the references on p. 64.

What important features of the story of Jesus are missing from Paul's picture? Why do you think Paul is silent about them?

> **He was descended from David according to the flesh and designated Son of God in power by his resurrection from the dead.**
>
> **He died for our sins in accordance with the scriptures, he was buried, he was raised on the third day in accordance with the scriptures, and he appeared to Cephas, then to the twelve. Then he appeared to more than five hundred brethren at one time, most of whom are still alive, though some have fallen asleep.**
>
> **On the night when he was betrayed he took bread, and when he had given thanks, he broke it and said, 'This is my body which is for you. Do this in remembrance of me.' In the same way also the cup, after supper, saying, 'This cup is the new covenant in my blood. Do this, as often as you drink it, in remembrance of me.'**
>
> **I saw none of the other apostles except James the Lord's brother.**

2 The New Testament Gospels

A few years later the first Gospels were written; they contain a good deal of material which had been handed down in story form by word of mouth, but this was not brought together in the Gospels until a generation after Jesus' death. There are four Gospels. Matthew, Mark and Luke belong quite closely together; John stands somewhat apart.

Although each of the Gospel writers produced his own portrait, years after the earthly life of Jesus, the material they used was not usually original. They probably reproduced many things which had been written in other documents or had been passed on by word of mouth (see above). Mark's was the first Gospel, and Matthew and Luke copied some passages from him almost word for word. However, because each writer was painting his own portrait, he would make small alterations here and there. You can see how from the parallel texts opposite:

Here are some important facts about the Gospels.

(*a*) The Gospels were written by Christians – that is, people who were committed to following Jesus and his Way. They are not newspaper reports or impartial histories (if you can have such things), but portraits, concerned to draw out the meaning of Jesus' life, death and resurrection. Each writer produces a distinctive portrait of Jesus by the way in which he arranges the material he has and the details he stresses. (See how many more of the sayings of Jesus appear in Matthew and Luke than in Mark.)

(*b*) None of the writers told the whole story. Whilst a great deal of material appears in more than one Gospel, much only appears in one place. (Look for yourself and see if you can find parables told only by Luke or miracles told only by John. Why do you think John has no account of the Last Supper like the others?)

John's Gospel stands very much apart in this respect, as you can see from his version of the same incident.

THE BAPTISM OF JESUS

Matt. 3.13–17	Mark 1.9–11	Luke 3.21–22
13 Then Jesus came from Galilee to the Jordan to John, to be baptized by him. John would have prevented him, saying, "I need to be baptized by you, and do you come to me?" But Jesus answered him, "Let it be so now; for thus it is fitting for us to fulfil all righteousness." Then he consented. And when Jesus was baptized, he went up immediately from the water, and behold, the heavens were opened and he saw the Spirit of God descending like a dove and alighting on him; and lo, a voice from heaven, saying, "This is my beloved Son, with whom I am well pleased."	9 In those days Jesus came from Nazareth of Galilee and was baptized by John in the Jordan. And when he came up out of the water, immediately he saw the heavens opened and the Spirit descending upon him like a dove; and a voice came from heaven, "Thou art my beloved Son; with thee I am well pleased."	21 Now when all the people were baptized and when Jesus also had been baptized and was praying, the heaven was opened, and the Holy Spirit descended upon him in bodily form, as a dove, and a voice came from heaven, "Thou art my beloved Son; with thee I am well pleased."

(c) In the portraits they painted, the Gospel writers not only wanted to tell their audience about what Jesus said and did. They were concerned about two other things.

1 Jesus was the fulfilment of the hopes and promises of the Old Testament, the Bible of the Jews among whom he came.

2 Hearing stories about Jesus would help people to follow him in the way.

3 Other Gospels

As time goes on, all kinds of stories cluster round famous figures, and Jesus was no exception here. Dozens of 'Gospels' appeared during the second century, some of them obviously little more than popular entertainment, or aimed at showing that Jesus was 'the greatest'. You can find these collected together in what is called *The Apocryphal New Testament*. We are told how, for example, Jesus cursed a child who bumped into him in the street, whereupon the child dropped down dead. Or how he would help Joseph by stretching planks which Joseph had cut too short.

Other 'apocryphal' Gospels are best understood as ways in which groups of new Christians tried to make sense of Jesus in terms of their own different experience and culture. One collection of such Gospels, so-called 'Gnostic Gospels', were found in 1945 in Nag Hammadi, in Egypt, having been lost since the second century AD. They show how some Christians attempted to interpret Jesus in a more 'spiritual' way.

4 Christians through Roman eyes

There is nothing suspicious in the fact that most of our information about Jesus comes from Christians, both in dominant groups and on the fringe. In the early days of Christianity there would have been little cause for non-Christian writers to mention him. However, there are some allusions in Roman literature.

Tacitus, writing about AD 116 of the persecution of Christians by Nero, regards the followers of Jesus and their religion as a 'pernicious superstition'. He tells us that their leader, Christus, was executed by Pontius Pilate in the reign of Tiberius.

Suetonius, a biographer of the same period, tells us that Claudius expelled the Jews from Rome because they constantly caused disturbances 'at the instigation of Chrestus'.

Pliny, a contemporary Roman governor, asks his emperor how to deal with Christians singing hymns to Christ 'as to a god'.

To sum up

What we know about Jesus and the first Christians comes from the New Testament, most prominent in which are the Gospels and the letters of Paul.

Once we begin to look further at the story of Jesus and the rise of the church, we find that it is quite complicated and that we do not know all the details (the New Testament is full of tantalizing allusions to events about which we are likely to remain ignorant).

What is in the New Testament is affected

    by the character, convictions and aims of the writers;
    by the different environments in which they worked;
    by their subject – Jesus: risen from death;
                    fulfilling Old Testament hopes;
                    initiating God's Kingdom.

Although some details of what happened may be unclear, what we do see are writers who have put their faith in Jesus as the one who announced a new age – the Kingdom of God – to be realized here and now; calling people to change their ways by allowing God to govern their lives. Everyone had cause to celebrate, because the reign of God was arriving. And yet, God demanded total obedience; and his claims were paramount.

Above all, Jesus was not just a figure of the past – he was a living Lord.

8 It's all in the Bible!

In the last chapter, we discussed the Bible sources which tell us about Jesus. As soon as the Bible is mentioned, arguments start! This happens simply because people do not agree about how we should use the church's special book.

1 Some people believe that the Bible is one of the supreme ways in which God has chosen to reveal himself. They argue that it must therefore be an accurate historical account of events which took place exactly as they are described: the Gospels, for example, are a completely reliable summary of what Jesus really said and did.

Those who take this view of the Bible claim they have an unquestionable, unshakable foundation for Christian believing and living today.

But this view has several weaknesses:

> It ignores the great diversity (and the obvious contradictions) within the Bible; for the more one reads it, the more one realizes that the Bible is not a simple and thoroughly consistent set of writings.
> It treats the whole Bible as permanently and universally valid; whereas the Bible contains much which cannot be abstracted from its historical context and treated like that without misleading and harmful consequences.

2 Some people believe that the Bible is primarily a collection of human responses to God, expressed in all kinds of ways: stories, poems, letters, myths, essays and dramatic constructions. In these writings, people recorded what they felt about God, determined, in the New Testament, by their knowledge of Jesus. At the end of the day – according to their understanding of the Bible – it doesn't matter whether particular parts are grounded in historical events. It is more important that we in turn make a personal response to God here and now, than to find out what precisely happened thousands of years ago, even if that were possible. Indeed some would say that to be obsessed with historical facts is a sign of a lack of faith!

The strength of this approach is that it emphasizes present faith and responding to God today in personal experience. Such a view is not undermined by discrepancies or uncertainties in the biblical record, which it fully accepts as part of the faith of the church.

But it has shortcomings, too:

> It can be too subjective: depending too much on personal opinions, insights and presuppositions.
> To make a personal belief the final authority is to say that truth equals whatever conclusion I reach; and however sincere I am, however rigorous my thinking, that is too simple and too arrogant!

3 Some people adopt a third approach to the Bible, which seeks to take both the others seriously, but without sharing their basic presuppositions. Such people agree that it is faith in God which comes first. But they also affirm that it is important to give proper attention to what really happened in the formative years of Christianity. By so doing, the Christian will be prevented from inventing his own fanciful doctrines. We may not be able to identify wholly with early views of Jesus, for they were attempts to present the gospel to particular people in a particular age. Today's Christians must find new ways and words to tell twentieth-century people about God. Such expressions must be related to the past, but not slavishly ruled by it.

This view sees belief in God as continuously developing, not abruptly arrested in a form it took centuries ago, but sometimes flowering, sometimes withering. It is rooted in the past, but it renews itself in the present. It responds to a God who draws near to people as significantly today as he did to Moses or Jesus.

> The disadvantage of this view is that it is not fixed by any ultimate authority, be it Bible, church, or individual experience. It is not final; its convictions are often blurred and qualified, for it perceives that tomorrow will bring more insights.

Such a view is both unsettling and invigorating!

More questions

1 Why is it that different groups, who each insist upon the infallible authority of the Bible as the final Word of God, do not agree among themselves on points of doctrine? e.g. members of 'conservative evangelical churches', Mormons, Jehovah's Witnesses?
2 It has been said that the story of Creation in Genesis is a myth: i.e. a story which, though imaginary, contains essentially true religious ideas. What do you think? Does it matter if some Bible accounts have no factual basis? Are there any New Testament stories that make more sense to you when thought of in this way?
3 Why is it that some Bible attitudes have been abandoned today? For example, why do we no longer execute adulterers or keep women quiet in church?

What do you think of the Bible?

Is it an infallible book in which the truth is unalterably fixed?

Is it an expression of people's faith, which has only a slender relationship to any known facts?

Is it a cumulative record of how real people in particular situations communicated their experience and ideas of God to their contemporaries, not tying us down to their views, but providing clues for our time as well?

Putting it into practice

Here are three complementary groups of questions that need to be raised when you set about the study of a biblical passage.

1 Examine the background. In each passage, members of the people of Israel or of the early church have written down what they believed God had taught them in their time and situation. Some of these questions will be appropriate:

> What sort of writing is it: a poem, a prayer, a historical record, a legal text, a letter, a story?
> Where and when did the event or conversation described take place?
> Who is speaking, who is listening, who else is there?
> What are the key terms and images that dominate the passage, and what did they mean to the writer?
> How have the writer's own situation and preoccupations affected his treatment of the material? (In the case of the Gospels, look at the parallel passages indicated with the section headings in the Good News Bible, or in footnotes in some other translations.)

2 In every generation, people have discovered in these writings something of God's purpose for men and women, society and the church:

> What similarities and contrasts are there between then and now?
> How could today be affected by the biblical story?
> What difference would it have made to the story if the writer had known what I know?
> What must the truth be, if it made people in that particular time and place respond to it in the way they did?

3 It is also valid to ask (perhaps even at the very beginning of the study) whether the passage in question rings any contemporary bells:

> Does anything in my own experience bring this story alive: something that's happened to me, or a recent news item?
> How does this story challenge me?
> Do I see myself, my attitudes, my relationships in a new light?

Sometimes the passage will vividly illuminate a contemporary issue or a personal problem; it will click with our experience. Other passages will not – the historical and literary study will have improved our knowledge but not our insight. For some biblical ideas have been left behind, and must be jettisoned in the search for truth.

9 Exploring the Gospels

Mark's Gospel

the earliest one to be written, about AD 65, portrays a Jesus

> who was given God's spirit at baptism
> who was called by God to announce the dawning of a new age
> who challenged people to change their ways and allow God to direct their lives
> who lived for God, who obeyed God, in such a way that he was called 'Son of God'.

It was entirely consistent with Mark's view of Jesus for him to report the Lord as saying, 'Why do you call me good? No one is good, but God!' For Mark, Jesus was the 'Christ' – the Greek word used to denote the Hebrew 'Messiah', or 'deliverer sent by God'. But Mark's picture of Jesus is a very human one, far from the pretentious statements of the creeds drawn up by Christians of later centuries.

John's Gospel

on the other hand, written about AD 90, is much closer in thought to the declaration of the Nicene Creed (AD 381): 'We believe in one Lord Jesus Christ, the only Son of God, eternally begotten of the Father, God from God, Light from Light, true God from true God.'

John spoke of Jesus

> as 'one with the Father'
> who was God's Word, through whom all things were made
> who was eternal, existing before he appeared on earth and living for ever.

It was entirely consistent with John's view of Jesus for him to report the Lord saying, 'I am the Way, the Truth and the Life; no one comes to the Father but by me'; or 'I and the Father are one'; or 'He who has seen me has seen the Father.'

Both John and Mark affirm the worth of Jesus, as the person through whom God will change the world and bring in a new age. But at the same time, they display marked differences in their assessment of Jesus himself. For each writer composed his own portrait of Jesus, drawing on the religious ideas and vocabulary of his own day. In this way they developed an understanding of Jesus which would make the greatest impact on their own churches.

Various theories have been proposed about the Gospels, attempting to establish the real-life situation in which each was written.

Matthew's Gospel

is thought by some to have been written by a converted Jewish scribe. He belonged to a group of Christians who still worshipped in the synagogue (the Jewish meeting house), reading the set scripture readings for each sabbath and festival in the Jewish calendar. During the sermons, the scribe commented upon these Jewish readings, using his own traditional teaching methods, and drawing on some remembered stories of Jesus. Eventually a sequence of such Christian comments upon the Jewish series of lessons was written down in what we call the 'Gospel of Matthew'. So we conceive the author as a devout Jewish Christian, who uses all his abilities and the tools of his trade to expound the meaning of Jesus to his fellow converts. Matthew uses a great deal of Mark's information, but he changes some of it and in so doing shows how he views things in a slightly different way.

> The request for a top place in the coming Kingdom (see Matthew 20.20–28 and Mark 10.25–45).
>
> Mark tells us that it was James and John who put the ambitious question to Jesus. Matthew puts the question in the mouth of their mother – a woman who makes no other appearance in the Gospels. Which version is more likely? Why would it be changed? Does it tell you anything about how Mark and Matthew viewed James and John?
>
> The stilling of the storm
> (see Matthew 8.23–27 and Mark 4.35–41).
>
> Mark tells us that the disciples accuse Jesus of not caring if they drown. How does Matthew's version differ? Why do you think he changed things? What does it say about his view of Jesus?

Whilst Matthew copied a great deal of Mark's Gospel, his ideas of Jesus and the disciples are more developed. Jesus is venerated as the One who fulfils Old Testament promises about a coming Messiah – someone who will save God's people from their enemies and establish God's eternal Kingdom. The disciples are Jesus' chief agents in his mission to the world.

Luke's Gospel

is said to have been written by a Gentile (a person who was not a Jew, and who was treated as an outcast by Jews). Hence his stress that Jesus is for everyone. He dated the beginning of his Gospel by the reigning Roman Emperor and the current Roman governor. He alone records the parable of the Good Samaritan, the story of the Samaritan healed of leprosy, and Jesus' statement that 'people will come from the east and the west, from the north and the south, and sit down at the feast in the Kingdom of God', while he omits Matthew's report that Jesus told the disciples not to go to the Samaritans or the Gentiles. He gives greater prominence than the other gospels to women, to the poor, to outcasts. In this way, Luke commends Jesus, not only as the Messiah of Israel, but also as God's gift to the world. (You will find references for all these passages on p. 64.)

Look again at the stilling of the storm passages in Matthew and Mark, and this time compare them with Luke 8.22–25. How does Luke report the incident?

In each case the finished Gospel represents

> the writer's response to his own cultural situation
> the kind of person he is
> his own perception of the message and ministry of Jesus as handed down in the Christian memory.

It's not surprising, therefore, that in many ways the Gospels agree, while in others they differ, in their view of Jesus. But they are united in their commitment to Jesus.

> He is the source of their Good News
> It is in response to his life and death and, above all, to his victory over death that they set out the Jesus story for their contemporaries
> For them, Jesus makes God 'real'.

The Gospels present four different portraits, but they were all inspired by the one Jesus.

10 Jesus in his day

In spite of the differences between the Gospels, can we piece together a basic outline of Jesus and his work? None of the criteria which scholars have devised for evaluating the historical likelihood of the New Testament records are entirely satisfactory, and there are many points of detail about which they would either disagree or admit that the evidence is insufficient. Yet there is considerable agreement about the general picture, the salient themes of his preaching, the impact of his work, the assessment of his character.

The most difficult issue is the place of the supernatural in the story. It is frequently argued today that 'because Jesus was different from us, because he was Son of God', there is no reason to doubt that his mother was a virgin, that shepherds saw angels at his birth, that he walked on the water, and rose from the dead.

But to argue like this is quite foreign to the approach of the Gospel writers. It is important to recognize that for them, belief in the miraculous formed part of their understanding of everyday life:

> Jesus wasn't the only one who could cast out devils. He wasn't the only one to perform miraculous healings.

> He wasn't the only one to rise from the dead – there were Old Testament precedents, as well as Lazarus and the widow's son at Nain.

> People like Ananias and Sapphira were punished by supernatural intervention too.

> Lots of people had visits from angels.

We do not share this way of looking at things. (We write off accounts of supernatural intervention we come across in Greek, or Nordic, or Hindu mythology as superstition.) What came naturally to the first-century writers is incongruous to us. We forget that their very view of the universe and of God's place in it was very different indeed from our own, with a firmament, a firm framework, keeping out the waters of chaos which were to be found above and below the earth.

In many ways, if we are to be true to the more comprehensive understanding of the world to which God has brought us over the centuries, then we must accept that the Gospel stories are coloured by a different world view and a different, often unscientific, understanding.

The Gospel writers interpreted events in terms of their own world view, and we could easily write them off at times as being merely superstitious. But this would be to dishonour them. As a man of his time, Jesus interpreted God's love in terms of his own world view. This does not render his life and teaching irrelevant; rather, it deepens our understanding, and spares us from simplistic conclusions.

A summary of the main features of Jesus' life and teaching:

1 Jesus believed that John the Baptist's remarkable one-man preaching mission heralded the dawn of a new age. He joined the crowds who flocked to hear John and was baptized by him. Soon he began to share in the proclamation himself. Jesus became a wandering preacher.

2 Jesus was a healer and exorcist. That is, he restored sick and handicapped people to health, and brought release to those oppressed by guilt and fear, by driving out devils.

3 Jesus called God 'Father' – in his own language, 'Abba'. He drew strength from this intimate relationship.

4 Jesus believed that he had a special vocation; that he was called by God, his Father, to bring in a new age. He called himself 'Son of Man', and his followers called him 'Messiah' – two of the Old Testament names given to the person sent by God to bring in a new Golden Age of peace and prosperity, when Israel would be free of her enemies.

5 Jesus gathered together a group of disciples, with whom he lived and shared his work. Some of these were social outcasts. Jesus welcomed them as followers, and he expected them to show the same concern for one another and for their enemies.

6 Jesus came into conflict with the old religion, with its emphasis on rules and laws. He believed that slavish obedience to the law had been superseded by love; it was more important to do good, and to act in a loving way, than to be obsessed by so many rules and regulations. As a result, he came into conflict with some of the most powerful people and groups in Jewish life, e.g. the Pharisees, lawyers (scribes) and priests.

7 Jesus came to see that he would be killed, but he believed that his death would bring in a new age. He spoke of this often, but especially at supper with his friends.

8 Shortly after his death, Jesus' disciples began to claim that he was alive. They said they had seen him — but even when he was not to be seen, they believed he was still with them. They were convinced that death was not the end of him. They claimed he had given them the gift of his Spirit — the Spirit which had entered Jesus at baptism — enabling them to live in his way. They invited others to join them and be baptized as followers and friends of Jesus.

Remember

1 The story of Jesus comes to us through the filter of human experience; from real people, trying to make sense of the Jesus-traditions in their own day, and using their own thought-forms.

2 Because of their different situations, the Gospel writers present different portraits of Jesus. So is it fair to invent a sort of amalgam of the stories from bits of the Gospels? Should we not simply accept diversity as part of life?

3 We are committed to the search for the historical Jesus; not so that we can copy him in a crude literalistic manner, but in order to develop a contemporary response to his message. In other words, we are aiming to do just what the first Christians did, when they allowed the Spirit of Jesus to draw from them new responses, and take them in new directions.

Once again, we are reminded of Christopher Columbus . . . the man who would not allow the past to become a fetish, but who was prepared to take a risk, believing that new truths would emerge, and new discoveries would be made.

11 Jesus in every generation

We have tried to understand the way in which his contemporaries looked at Jesus and what they saw in him.
Between them and us stand two thousand years. How have people down the centuries responded to the story of Jesus?

Make a list of people who have shown in their lives the qualities Jesus exemplified, such as compassion and friendship, drive and determination, love of truth and trust in God.

Who would you include and why?

Not only famous people, but people you have known personally;

Not only people now dead, but people still living; living in the way of Jesus today.

A few suggestions
(*if you would like to find out more about these people, look in your library for biographies*).

Elizabeth Fry (1780–1845)

A philanthropic Quaker, wife of a London merchant and mother of a large family. Her campaign for prison reform, and her welfare work amongst women prisoners and other classes of the destitute and helpless, was motivated by a strong Christian impulse.

Matteo Ricci (1552–1610)

A Jesuit missionary who was the first European to gain access to the forbidden city of Pekin. Because he was willing to adopt Chinese ways, he was able to win the friendship of the Emperor and toleration for Chinese Christians.

Francis of Assisi (1182–1226)

He took Matthew 10.7–9 literally and lived the life of a wandering preacher and friend of the poor.

John Wesley (1703–1791)

An Anglican minister who travelled tirelessly for half a century to preach especially to the poor and uneducated working people. He pioneered the development of small groups for mutual support, with local leaders to follow up his work.

Martin Luther King (1929–1968)

A Baptist minister and champion of civil rights for black people in the USA. He kept to non-violent principles throughout the struggle, but was himself assassinated.

Mother Teresa of Calcutta (1910–)

A Yugoslavian nun, who left her teaching Order to live and work amongst the poor in the slums of Calcutta. Her Sisters of Charity now care for abandoned children, the sick and the dying in cities throughout India and other parts of the world.

Remember, too, that the concerns which Jesus – and Christians after him – have stood for have motivated not only individuals but movements, some of them not specifically Christian, to serve their own generation, right down to the present day.

See what you can find out about the organizations whose symbols appear on this page.

So much for a few suggestions . . . now make your own list.

If you cannot identify some of the symbols you will find the organizations listed on page 64.

12 Jesus our contemporary

The historical study of Jesus opens the way to questions about his significance for today's world. Is he just a figure from the past, whose story has no relevance for us; or does his approach to living make sense in our experience?

In this chapter, we identify some of the convictions that were central to Jesus' way of life – beliefs and attitudes which demand a response from us.

Jesus believed that this is God's world

Everyone is a child of God (even people we don't like).
Jesus believed that everything and everyone is God's business. Remember the priest and the temple servant, who were too pre-occupied to help a stranger?
We belong to one another. There's more to life than simply pursuing personal ends.

What does this say about race relations?
How does being a Christian affect your choice of a job?

Jesus had a mixed bunch of friends

They were not all fishermen! They included a freedom fighter (Simon the Zealot), a man who collected taxes for the Roman occupying forces (Matthew), and a woman who lived a pretty doubtful sort of life. Whatever his family ties, he still spent time with others; even unsavoury and unpopular characters, and simple and needy people. Yet he was sought out by leaders, rich and respectable people, and even an army captain.
Is the church as open to all kinds of people as Jesus was?
What would happen if a prostitute came to join your church or group?
How would you react to a millionaire who joined the church?

Jesus believed that there is a purpose in life

God's will is that people should live in unity and peace with one another; this is what Jesus meant by the Kingdom of God, i.e. the 'government' of God. So we work and pray for a day when everything and everyone will be united 'on earth as in heaven'.

List some of the discoveries and inventions of recent times.

Which of them serve God's creative purpose?
Which have been used to thwart it?
How can the capacity of the human spirit for understanding, sensitivity, and love be developed?

Jesus had a simple life-style

He believed that life is to be enjoyed, but his pleasures were simple.
His stories show his delight in observing the ways of men and women.
He enjoyed parties and meals too. On the other hand, Jesus took no pleasure in material wealth just for its own sake. Riches would not secure a man's future. 'If you want to learn from me,' he said, 'then forget yourself and follow me.'

Is it possible for a twentieth-century Western Christian to copy Jesus' simple life-style?
How, in practice, can you go about it?

Jesus cared for people

This was the hall-mark of Jesus' life. The well-being of others was supremely important; more so than rules and regulations. He was known as one to whom people with all kinds of problems could turn for help; and this selfless love of his was infectious.

What individuals and groups around you care for others in the way Jesus did?
What place does concern for others have in your church's programme?
Is there something you can do for somebody?

Jesus called God 'Father'

It was a surprise to the Jews to hear Jesus call God 'Abba' (Father); the nearest word we have to 'Abba' is 'Daddy' or 'Dad'. The Jews believed that God is unapproachable, yet Jesus treated God as a constant companion, to whom he looked for strength.
At crucial moments in his life, Jesus made special arrangements to spend time in prayer, but prayer was also a natural part of his life.

What word most expresses your relationship to God?
'Father', 'Daddy', 'Mother', 'Creator', 'Almighty', 'Eternal Spirit', 'Lord', . . . or what?

Jesus was ready to suffer for what he believed

The friends of Jesus found it very hard to accept that following him meant self-denial and even suffering. Over and over again, Jesus failed to make them understand what was the true nature of his vocation. He was not a powerful princely figure, but rather a servant, unprotected from exploitation and abuse.

List some Christians who have followed the way of suffering.

What would you have done in their place?
Can you think of any situation in which to remain faithful to Jesus you would have to suffer?

This way of Jesus is no soft option. It's costly.

It's the way Jesus lived himself; here's how Alan Dale describes Jesus:

> He was sincere in all he did; he knew what he stood for; he could put up with anything; he was very kind; he didn't just talk about loving people – he actually succeeded in loving them; he always told people the plain truth; for he knew God was with him and trusted God's power.

Living like that led to execution for Jesus on a Roman cross. But afterwards the disciples discovered that the secret of life was to live as he had lived; selflessly, sacrificially, lovingly.

Don't be persuaded to believe that following the way of Jesus is simple and straightforward. We'll sometimes be driven into doubt, and even despair. This is the cost of discipleship. The miracle is that God will still be creating new possibilities, even whilst we are still in darkness.

13 The disciples of Jesus: then and now

He said 'Follow me'

He came, almost out of nowhere, to a variety of ordinary people, and interrupted them at what they were doing. He came to Peter and Andrew, James and John, on the lakeshore, and summoned them to be fishers of men. He came to Matthew, the tax collector, and to half a dozen or so others, and to all of them he said, 'Follow me'. He comes to ordinary people today, men and women, no matter what they may be doing, and the call is the same: 'Follow me'.

He asked a great deal of them

He challenged them to turn away from evil, and allow God to govern their lives.

He expected them to care deeply about one another, to forgive those who hurt and insulted them, and to love both neighbours and enemies alike.

He knew they didn't understand everything. In fact what he asked was so hard that they constantly misunderstood, even after quite a long time, though they remained disciples.

He didn't only call respectable people; in fact he said that they didn't need him. He was concerned for the disreputable – and that wasn't easy to take.

He offered them a great deal

He wanted people to enjoy life at its best, responding to the love of God.

Through his work of teaching and healing, he brought hope, life and wholeness, when the world around seemed under the dominion of death, demons and decay.

When people were with him, life was often like a party, and he was often to be found at parties given by others.

He did not hold himself back in any way; in the end, what he offered to people was no less than himself.

He spent a lot of time with them

'Following' really meant going where he led them – around and about in Galilee, and south to Jerusalem. They listened hard and long to his words; they observed his ways; they learned to draw strength from God.

> What words of Jesus mean the most to you?
> How are his ways relevant to twentieth-century life?
> How do we receive strength from God?
> How much time do you give to your 'friendship with Jesus' – listening, praying, working it out?

He involved them in his work

He gave them jobs to do, tackling the evil powers at work in the world; superstition, greed, disease. So, even when they were not at his side, they were following his instructions and his example.

> What kind of work should we be involved in?
> List the different forms of Christian action to which people or groups you know are committed.
> What do you do?

He shared a special meal with them

Christians still follow the command of Jesus to eat bread and drink wine 'in remembrance' of him. This meal is known by many names: Lord's Supper, Eucharist, Holy Communion, Mass, Breaking of Bread. Sometimes it has united Christians, often it has bitterly divided them; while some Christians do not have a special meal, because they believe that every meal is a gift of God, where Jesus is present.

> What do you think of this 'meal'?
> Which of its names means most to you?

The church: A disciple-group

Following is not a lone activity. If we follow Jesus we are part of a world-wide company of fellow-travellers. Some of them are people to whom we are naturally attracted, others are people whose company we would never have sought. The call to follow is a call to team up with them:

> to *celebrate* and worship God;
> to *support* one another in daily life;
> to put the way of Jesus into *action*.

Celebration

For many people, 'going to church' means attending a 'service', usually on a Sunday. Of course, there is far more than that to 'church' – and to Christian 'service'.

But it is true that the most distinctive feature of the life of the church is not its social evenings or business meetings or study groups or doing something to help others – such activities are found in other walks of life. The characteristic activity of the church is meeting for 'worship'; celebrating the love of God, sharing the good news of what he is doing, remembering Jesus – something to make a song and dance about! At its best, Christian celebration is an opportunity for everybody to share joys, hopes, concerns . . .

Think of a service you have attended which stands out in your memory as a real celebration. Why? What could be done to make services more joyful?

Suggest ways in which people could be more actively involved in your Sunday celebrations.

Support

Once people have come together for celebration in this way, it is unthinkable that they should separate until next time and do nothing further together. A 'church' is a community of people:

> who are engaged together in learning more about themselves, about the world, about the way of Jesus;
> who support one another as they try to live in the way of Jesus and reflect together on how it works out;
> who sustain, encourage, comfort each other in times of crisis.

Like any other human association this presupposes some measure of organization.

Some churches are very highly structured, with various tiers of administration, innumerable committees, etc.

Others claim to be more loosely organized, though in practice that often means a few people taking all the decisions!

However complex or slight the organization, it is important to remember that the church is essentially a *movement* rather than an *institution*. It exists for the sake of people, not for its own sake.

What opportunities are there in your church
for exploring and learning?
for sharing?
for outsiders to join?

Are there people around to
whom you can turn for
support?
Who?

Action

Sooner or later, the Christian life (and the credibility of the church) stands or falls by its ability to inspire Christian deeds: practical involvement in everyday affairs. A church which ignores the world around is irrelevant. But the question 'What is the *church* doing in the community? means 'What are the *Christians* doing, either singly or in groups?'

Try and identify an immediate concern to which you can respond in the spirit of Jesus. Ask yourself, 'If Jesus came to this area, who would he get involved with?' or 'How can I put love into action?' – the ultimate test of discipleship.

Then he needs encouragement and help so that he can provide for himself.

What does a hungry man need?

He needs friends who will give him a square meal.

And he probably needs some radical changes made in the structure of society, if he is never to go hungry again.

In other words, Christian actions are of various kinds, including:

> Immediate, practical help to people in difficulty or distress; picking up the pieces, binding up the wounds, 'casualty' work amongst the victims of disease or of other people's misdeeds or of society's neglect. There are unlimited opportunities for this form of Christian service.

> Constant, caring support for people at different stages of life: play-groups, youth clubs, old people's centres (not 'casualty', but 'therapy').

> Attacking the root causes that underlie many a tragedy: the injustices and inequalities that abound in society ('preventive medicine'). This means engaging in the political struggle for a society where everyone gets a fair deal, where everyone's right to be heard is respected, and where the rights of future generations are preserved.

Take the call to action seriously, and you are likely to find yourself in unexpected company: people who owe no allegiance to Jesus, but who share some of his concern for the world and his insight as to what needs changing.

It is a temptation to stand aloof from them, to treat people with different views or religions from your own as enemies, fools, or heretics; to be sectarian and exclusive. But it is likely that you can learn from them; they may possess some precious insights you have missed. Our calling is to love others as much as we love ourselves. That means:

> Treating people seriously, by being open to their ideas and their way of life.
>
> Learning from other faiths and Christian denominations.
>
> Seizing every opportunity to join with people of goodwill to work for the common good.

Making a start

Jesus' ministry began with his baptism. He joined up with others who wanted to demonstrate to everyone that they had finished with the old selfish way of life.

They changed direction and began to live in a new way.
Just as John the Baptist had baptized those who wanted to make a new start, so did the first Christians. Often, this involved being immersed in water, to symbolize both the washing and the death of the old self. It was a new person who emerged.

Baptism is still practised today, as a sign that someone is setting out to live in God's way.

When children are baptized, they cannot articulate their feelings, nor can they promise to follow in the way of Jesus; nevertheless, it is the beginning of their life in the family of the church. At baptism, we proclaim God's love for them, and pray that through life they will follow the leadership of Jesus.

As the years go by, young disciples are nurtured and encouraged until a time when they decide for themselves to follow in the way of Jesus. In many churches, such a decision is marked publicly by confirmation or reception into membership. In others, baptism itself takes place at this time.

Have you been baptized? What does it mean to you?

What does Jesus' call, 'Follow me', mean for you now?

14 Programme for tomorrow

In this book, you have been bombarded with *questions* . . . about yourself . . . your group . . . the world . . . Jesus . . . the Bible . . . the church . . . and so on . . .

Questions . . . questions . . . questions!

A mature person is someone who can live with the questions which life brings, rather than run away from them – even when there are no simple answers.

Such a person can face uncertainty with hope;
> act confidently, even when the way ahead is clouded;
> follow the way of Jesus, without always understanding everything;
> find strength to live positively, even when stress and suffering have to be endured.

Similarly, a mature church or group is one which lives creatively with questions: it's an 'enquiring community' of people committed to the search for truth. Here they will find sympathy, understanding and acceptance; but not necessarily agreement. Argument, and even conflict, can be fruitful and creative. To stifle disagreement is to stunt growth and restrict development.

> Is your group a clique, full of self-satisfied and like-minded people?
> Or are you open to others?

> Are you prepared to change to accommodate other people?
> Or do you expect them to fit in with your ideas?

There are times when attitudes are more important than ideas and dogmas.

Open to the future

If we proceed towards tomorrow in a spirit of discovery, we may find that we have to revise some of our assumptions.

1 How can we best talk about Jesus?

   In a way which is true *for us*; but which is also true *to him*; and will mean something *to other people*.

2 How can the church best respond to the message of Jesus?

   In its worship celebrations?
   What about liturgies (i.e. forms of service, hymns, prayers, etc)? Are they intelligible? Do they say the right things? Has tradition become an end in itself? Do we need different kinds of worship for different people?

   In its activities?
   Do we spend our time doing the right things? What ought we to be doing for one another, for other people, near and far?

   In its organization?
   Who makes the plans and takes the decisions? Does everyone feel involved? Do the buildings, committees, and functions help people to live in the way of Jesus? How is the church's money obtained and spent? Have we got our priorities right?

3 How does following Jesus affect the way we live?

   the company we keep?
   how we earn our money?
   how we use it . . . house, car, holidays, other people, the poor?

The big question about tomorrow is . . .

Is the way of Jesus significant enough to change things for
   you
   your group
   your church
   your world?

If the answer is 'yes'

then start writing a programme for tomorrow:

A programme prompted by God's Spirit

> creatively working in the world – making all things new; active in human life, renewing our strength and our hope, binding us to one another;
> the spirit that filled Jesus – the one who makes God real.

It will mean

A personal commitment:

> to go on seeking the answers to your questions and the fulfilment of your aspirations;
> to which you can give yourself honestly and completely.

A commitment to others:

> joining with them to celebrate the love of God;
> to learn together about the way of Jesus;
> to support one another at all times;
> to share in Christian work.

A commitment to the world and its people:

> some enjoy its riches and its beauty;
> others wait in misery for a better day.

A commitment to the way of Jesus:

> 'I believe that this is God's world;
> I believe that there is a purpose in life;
> I have a mixed bunch of friends;
> I have a simple life-style;
> I care for people;
> I call God "Father",
> I am ready to suffer for what I believe in.'

'One more step along the world I go . . .'

References

The extracts from Paul's letters on p. 29 are taken from Romans 1.3; I Corinthians 15.3–6; 11.23–25; Galatians 1.19.

The quotations on p. 37 are from Mark 10.17f.; John 1.1–15; 14.6–10; 10.30.

The passages in Luke's Gospel referred to on p. 38 are: 2.1f.; 10.30–37; 17.11–19; 13.29.

The passages referred to on p. 40 are: Luke 9.49; Acts 5.15f.; 19.13–16; 28.8f.; II Kings 4.34; John 11.44; Luke 7.14f.; Acts 5.1–10.

References on pp. 48ff. are as follows:
Jesus believed that this is God's world: Matthew 5.43–48; Luke 10.30–35; 16.19–31.
Jesus had a mixed bunch of friends: Matthew 10.2–4; Luke 7.36–39; Mark 3.31–35; Matthew 9.10–13; Luke 15.1–7; 14.12–24; 7.1–10; John 3.1.
Jesus believed that there is a purpose in life: Matthew 5.3–10, 23f.; 6.10.
Jesus had a simple life-style: Luke 13.18f.; 15.8–32; 12.32–34; Matthew 6.25; 8.20.
Jesus cared for people: Mark 10.21; 3.1–5; 14.1–5; 19.8.
Jesus called God 'Father': Luke 11.2; 10.21–24; Mark 1.35; Luke 9.28; Mark 14.32.
Jesus was ready to suffer rather than abandon God's way: Mark 8.31–38; 9.30–32; John 13.1–17.

The passages referred to on p. 56 are: Luke 7.18–22; I John 3.17; 4.16; James 2.15f.

The organizations whose symbols are reproduced on page 47 are
(reading from left to right and top to bottom):

Christian Aid
The World Development Movement
Amnesty International
The Samaritans
Shelter
The Imperial Cancer Research Fund
Oxfam
The Save the Children Fund
International Voluntary Service
National Society for the Prevention of Cruelty to Children
Christian Action

The publishers are grateful to the following for permission to reproduce illustrations on the pages shown:

19 E.W. Tattersall (Wesley Memorial Church)
24 The Mansell Collection (The Mona Lisa)
27 The Mansell Collection (portrait by Holman Hunt)
    The National Gallery (El Greco)
    Ernst Barlach
    Courtauld Institute of Art (Georges Rouault)
    Schweizerisches Landesmuseum, Zurich
45 The Mansell Collection (Matteo Ricci)
45 BBC Hulton Picture Library (Elisabeth Fry)
46 The Mansell Collection (St Francis of Assisi)
46 Camera Press (Martin Luther King, Mother Teresa)
46 Methodist Recorder (John Wesley)
    The Sydney Carter song *One More Step* on page 6 is used by kind permission of Stainer and Bell Ltd and the Galaxy Music Corporation.